To our wonderful G.G. Mom Grandma & G.G. Mom on her 85th Birthday. The photography in this book is all by Virginia Dixon, who did the girls pictures. The thoughts all very uplifting. One of the quotes says that our Blessings brighten when we count them, and on your 85th Birthday we are definitely counting you! We love you and are thankful for having you as one of our blessings.

Love Always,

Your Granddaughter

Liz

Grandma

Liz, Tom, Brooke, Erica & Brian

September 16, 1997

TENDER THOUGHTS

PHOTOGRAPHY COPYRIGHT © 1996 BY VIRGINIA DIXON

TEXT COPYRIGHT © 1996 BY GARBORG'S HEART 'N HOME, INC.

DESIGN BY MICK THURBER

PUBLISHED BY GARBORG'S HEART 'N HOME, INC.

P.O. BOX 20132, BLOOMINGTON, MN 55420

❧

❧

❧

❧

JANET L. WEAVER WISHES TO THANK JOAN M. GARBORG FOR HER EDITORIAL

DIRECTION AND WENDY GREENBERG FOR HER "APPLES OF GOLD."

ISBN 1-881830-30-6

Tender Thoughts

Photography by Virginia Dixon *with featured sentiments by* Janet L. Weaver

Look for the heaven here on earth. It is all around you.

Into all our lives, in many simple, familiar ways, God

infuses an element of joy from the surprises of life,

which unexpectedly brighten our days,

and fill our eyes with light.

....

LONGFELLOW

Joy is the heart's harmonious response to the Lord's

song of love.

....

A. W. TOZER

Every morning
is a fresh
opportunity to
find God's
extraordinary
joy in the
most ordinary
places.

Tenderness makes the journey precious.

How happy I am that I can walk beside you, lean on you, and live in the warmth of your friendship.

Good company on a journey makes the way seem shorter.

Life is short and we never have enough time for the hearts of those who travel the way with us. O, be swift to love! Make haste to be kind.

HENRI FRÉDÉRIC AMIEL

There is no safer place than the Father's hands.

Little deeds of kindness, little words of love,

Help to make earth happy like the Heaven above.

....

JULIA FLETCHER CARNEY

All of God's creatures are held in the hands of His kindness.

Prayer
lights the
pathway
to peace.

Like the summer breezes playing,

like the tall trees softly swaying,

Like the lips of silent praying,

is the perfect peace of God.

....

MICHAEL PERRY

Peace, hope, and comfort bloom in the garden of prayer.

The secret of life is that all we have and are is a gift of grace to be shared.

....

LLOYD JOHN OGILVIE

Whatever we have is worth twice as much when we share it.

*Friendship is a gift from God
that's blessed in every part...
born through love and loyalty...
conceived within the heart.*

Sharing with
another is a
simple way
to say...
we need
each other.

Faith believes that God will plant the seeds of hope for tomorrow in the garden of our hearts today.

All the flowers of tomorrow are in the seeds of today.

Faith makes all things possible. Hope makes all things bright. Love makes all things easy.

Now faith is being sure of what we hope for and certain of what we do not see.

....

HEBREWS 11:1 NIV

Blessings brighten
when we count them.
The more we look
for them, the more
of them we will see.

....

Maltbie D. Babcock

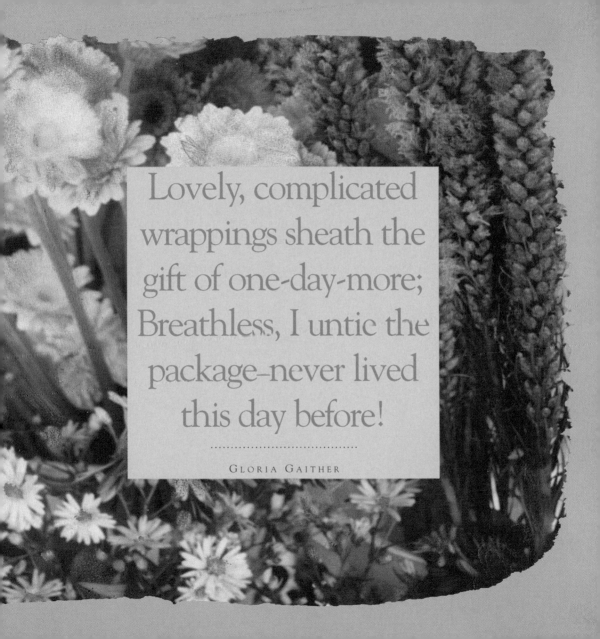

Lovely, complicated
wrappings sheath the
gift of one-day-more;
Breathless, I untie the
package–never lived
this day before!

GLORIA GAITHER

What the dew is to the flower, gentle words are to the soul.

Gentleness opens in each heart a little heaven.

We can make up our minds whether our lives in this world

shall…be beautiful and fragrant like the lilies of the field.

....

FATHER ANDREW SDC

*Gentleness is
the soil from
which tender
buds of love
open to share
their fragrance.*

The treasure our heart searches for is found in the ocean of God's love.

Love is the reason behind everything God does.

The earth is filled with his tender love.

·······································

PSALM 33:5 TLB

Everything we do is a portrait of ourselves. All our actions take their hue from the complexion of the heart.

Living the truth in your heart without compromise brings kindness into the world.

All that is worth cherishing begins in the heart.

The most delightful picture of humility is painted with the pure brush strokes of the heart.

Honesty
makes us
real in a
world of
pretend.

True worth is in being, not seeming—

in doing, each day that goes by, some little good—

not in dreaming of great things to do by and by.

....

ALICE CARY

Truth is such a rare thing, it is delightful to tell it.

....

EMILY DICKINSON

Faith goes up
the stairs that love
has made and looks
out of the windows
which hope has
opened.

·····························

CHARLES H. SPURGEON

All I have seen
teaches me to trust
the Creator for all I
have not seen.

RALPH WALDO EMERSON

A friend is a close companion on rainy days,

someone to share with through every phase…

Forgiving and helping to bring out the best, believing

the good and forgetting the rest.

If you love someone you will be loyal to [them]

no matter what the cost.

....

1 CORINTHIANS 13:7 TLB

A friend is someone who loves you as you are.

A loyal friend
always holds to
what is lovely
within us and
overlooks our
shortcomings.

*The tender
blossoms of the
heart make a
perfect bouquet
of hope…
May a garden
of hope always
bloom in
your heart.*

Friends…they cherish each other's hopes. They
are kind to each other's dreams.

We all mold one another's dreams. We all hold each other's
fragile hopes in our hands. We all touch each other's hearts.

Whenever I think of you, I smile inside.